SOUL Improvement

Mike Taylor

PEAKE ROAD

ISBN-1-57312-044-8

Soul Improvement

Mike Taylor

Copyright © 1996
Peake Road

6316 Peake Road
Macon, Georgia 31210-3960
1-800-747-3016

Peake Road
is an imprint of
Smyth & Helwys Publishing, Inc.®

All rights reserved.
Printed in the United States of America.

The paper used in this publication meets the minimum
requirements of American Standard for Information
Sciences—Permanence of Paper for Printed Library Material.
ANSI Z39.48–1984.

Library of Congress Cataloging-in-Publication Data

Taylor, Mike.
    Soul improvement / Mike Taylor.
    iv + 92 pp.   5.5 "x 7.5" (13.97 x 19.05 cm)
    Chiefly cartoons. I. Title.
    ISBN 1-57312-044-8 (alk. paper)
    NC1429.T374A4   1996
    741.5'973–dc20

                                      95-48120
                                         CIP

Editor's Note

Christians are a people who take the Bible seriously. Because we value it as a source of understanding who God is and what God wants for us, we also take seriously the persons met within the Scriptures.

Unfortunately, we sometimes allow our appreciation for the Scriptures to obscure our view of the joy, gladness, and humor found within those pages. As certainly as God created persons, these persons were created with a sense of humor. That sense of humor is good for our souls and comes from God. It keeps us balanced and keeps us from becoming so serious that we lose the playfulness of life intended by our creator.

In the cartoons of *Soul Improvement*, Mike Taylor reminds us of one of the central truths of the Bible—that God has a habit of taking the most unlikely of persons and situations and using them for wonderful purposes. He helps us laugh for joy as we realize that Noah, Moses, and David were real people used by God.

May your soul be lifted as you enjoy the humor of these cartoons; and thank God that, as silly as you and I often feel, God may well use us for a grander mission than we expect.

Adam names the animals.

Adam did perform a great act of faith.

The first word Adam said when he saw Eve

Some people believe that soon after Adam and Eve ate the apple, God created snow.

Like Adam, most men never forget their wife's first home-cooked meal.

Eve's favorite recipe book

Though Abel was a practical joker, one too-many spitballs pushed Cain over the edge.

Even though he was bald and 960 years-old, Methuselah still had to get a trim every now and then.

As a kid, Noah loved bath time.

God was preparing Noah early on.

When Shem was just a kid,
Noah was over 500 years-old.

But how am I supposed to build a boat?

Noah's ideas were eventually rejected.

Noah was the first insurance salesman.

Unfortunately, the dinosaurs decided to attend the Jurassic Expo that was held the same weekend that Noah loaded up the animals.

The first "bon voyage"

Noah was a good steward.

After awhile, the weather forecasts were a little depressing.

Noah's duties

Pork chops were the first meal on the ark.

Noah's favorite bedtime snack

Noah on latrine duty

The "Lurp Hounds'" last meal on earth

Noah spent four hours a day cleaning his sandals.

Noah and the animals get seasick.

Noah fell asleep on deck only one time during the cruise. Fortunately, it did turn into a deep tropical tan.

Mona always felt awkward squirtin' milk in a coffee cup.

Noah taking a long shower

It was an honor to be invited to sit in the captain's tub.

A move he would eventually regret, Noah put the polar bears in charge of freezer inventory.

Standard issue on the ark

Some theologians say Noah was a pretty good water skier.

There was never a dull moment on the ark due to Noah's three sons, Shem, Ham, and Japheth.

Moments before Noah would wake up and feed the animals

Noah, alias Captain Hook

After the sponge incident, Shem was permanently assigned to latrine duty during the entire voyage.

On that fateful day, the cowelephant became an endangered species, and playing fetch with the animals on the ark was forbidden.

After 40 days and nights on the ark, Noah and the crew get some well deserved R & R.

When the elephants started to dance, most everybody would get seasick.

Crisis on the Ark

A few of Noah's most cherished inventions

Noah took extra precautions on the ark.

Noah goes to the dentist.

After the pillar-of-salt incident, Lot eventually stopped taking his wife out to eat.

It wasn't just the coat of many colors that made Joseph's brothers jealous; it was that snappy pair of argyle socks.

Jethro was Moses' father-in-law.

No, it's not the burning bush; it's Moses at the age of 119, blowing out the candles on his birthday cake.

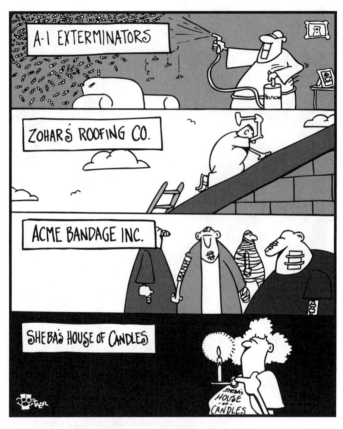

Business actually picked up some during the plagues of locusts, hail, boils, and darkness.

Moses was starting to get creative with his plagues on Pharaoh and Egypt.

Moses has to start over.

Let's face it. In the dry desert all that time, Moses probably had to do this a time or two.

Moses and his other staff

After wandering in the desert and eating manna for 40 years, Clem and Flem make an interesting discovery while cleaning Moses' tent.

Moses' great-grandson, Gomer, went on to become the best mechanic in town.

Moses taking a shower

One reason it took Moses 40 years to cross the desert

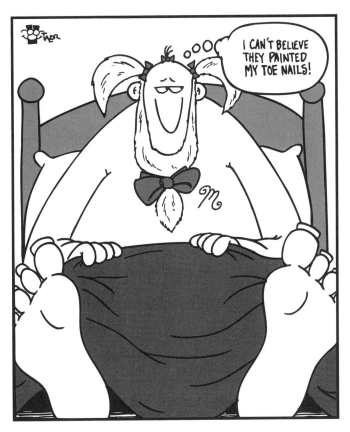

Moses' sons loved to play practical jokes on their dad.

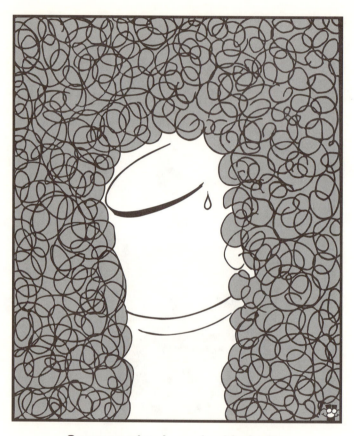

Sampson having a bad hair day

Sampson going for a walk on a windy day

The day Goliath was born

What was going on in David's mind just before he slew Goliath

Just after he cut if off, David spiked Goliath's head and was carried off the field by his teammates.

Every kid in Israel wanted one.

David eventually earned "Best Defensive Player of the Year."

About the time David was writing the book of Psalms, he came up with the idea of toilet paper.

Daniel was blessed with great wisdom.

Knowing that this wouldn't be their last meal, Shadrach, Meshach, and Abednego ordered hot dogs and marshmallows.

Back in the old days before they invented the Roman chariot windshield

Esther was considered a very beautiful woman; of course, no one ever heard of a Daisy shaver for women back then.

Jonah writes a "bestselling" scroll about a whale named Mobey.

Only the best gladiators got the endorsements.

Many people felt that the gladiator games were becoming too commercialized.

If not for the referees, things would have gotten out of hand.

Larry, the royal janitor for King James, goes to great extremes to get his book published.

First ad for a personal injury attorney

In protest for making the troops wear skirts, Thamulus gives King Herod a curtsy instead of the traditional chest salute.

It was the 70s . . . B.C.
Long hair, sandals, and of course
bell bottoms were in.

Huz and Buz were actually brothers mentioned in the Bible. Huz eventually became a barber and named a haircut in honor of his brother.

Tap Dancing B.C.
Of course, this was before tap shoes
and toenail clippers were invented.

Camelpooling to work

Some of the first recipients of honorary degrees

For awhile, the double knit leisure robe was the fashion rage for businessmen in all Israel.

Roman road-kill.

The biggest grand opening in the history of the Red Sea Surf Shop franchise

Hot Wheels!

One gust of wind eventually inspired Levi to invent bluejeans.